The
Beaver
Pond

Poems by

Benjamin
Rozonoyer

darkly bright press

The Beaver Pond
Poems by Benjamin Rozonoyer

Catalog Number 022

ISBN: 979-8-9899449-6-5

Library of Congress Control Number: 2024950595

darkly bright
press & design

www.darklybrightpress.com

Table of Contents

The
Beaver
Pond

Poems by

Benjamin
Rozonoyer

darkly bright press

To Eryn and Ita

Proem

.

The tale gets told upstairs,
where the standing horses sleep:
one can see the well is deep
when the muddy water clears.

A word which one lets go,
like a pebble, dropped, forms rings,
and sinks, and speaks below
of world-without-end things.

Upstairs, the horses snort,
and, swatting tails, they wake
from an egret of some sort
in the fog upon the lake.

Soapstone

Heretofore,
relinquishing quintessential habits,
I scaled mountains,
I talked to rabbits,
lived among rabbits.

Heaven
espied the earth—
its glimpse is the sky
of unprecedented size,
which is why
babies cry at birth.

The sides
of the rock
are slippery,
you have to knock—
a knocker of yew
or hickory
will let you in.

The wind—perpetual Rabbit-jostle,
a monotony making one's head to oscillate,
and fossil
solidify fossil
for as far as prairie and sky conflate.

A bird a bird,
even in the nethermost.
Look upon us Lord,
skim my speckled feathers.

Your words a kettleful,
your speech as if of steam.
Better steer your hull
towards the ever-running stream.

Whose life—hoplite?—fleet,
upon feet but half-long,
will land among the wheat
which one separates the chaff from?

I pledge the sea is large;
in it flash the plashing fish.
March along the ridge
overgrown with underbrush.

Sun Person

Look through the crack at the splintery light!
Lean to the wood if you have any sense—
Sun Person's dancing behind the fence.

Follow his footsteps that blink so bright,
sweeping inside and aside with glee;
what can you tell me?
he's catching light,
Pricking the ribs of a restless sea.

Look at the land that his eyes have charred—
what's all that noise?
did you hear him shout?
Nettles of prickthorn that hurt the heart,
threads of old summer like wandering trout.

Stifle the sobbing and step away!
swallow the teardrops and get thee hence—
it is Sun Person's body beside the fence.

Morning lure—
a whiff of manure.
Tomorrow's New Year
will make things newer
and today last year:

Snow in the pasture
amidst cornhusk-stubble—
yellow is humble.

Cottonwoods grow
on the side of the road,
where the Front Range is—
neighbors and strangers.

Put on a Carhartt—
become incarnate.

Throw a glance my way
and walk to the highway,
past the snow flurries—
cottonwood-worries.

In search for a word (for the Word is sinless),
I listened to different sorts of stillness.

It aches and it locks us painfully,
For He wakes and walks spontaneously.

...

I have heard it from hearsay
about McPherson
that he's fallen into a heresy
and is a different person.

At the moment we saw him plummet,
In the minute he smiled insanely,
We were seeking to see the summit,
We were starting to find him saintly.

When his needs became dire,
and his limbs feeble,
A ray framed our spire,
light gilded the steeple.

...

"This frame of flesh is thinning,
which joy must visit seldom—
We thought you were the elder,
we thought you were still living."

"If you look upon my face,
and see that it's aflame,
forget my name,
and leave me in this place."

"We see it aflame
with a spark of lust;
we'll leave if we must,
but remember your name,

"And in dry weather
offer up a prayer
that the clouds may gather,
layer upon layer."

...

Then the desert groaned with loneliness
at the memory of holiness,
at the imminence of illness.

Poet's Seat Tower, Greenfield, Massachusetts
Dedicated to Frederick Goddard Tuckerman (1821-1873)

Park the car as far
as the asphalt-end,
at the pathway-wend
toward the hill-top tower.

Greenfield on a grid,
aperture of arc.
Fix your eyes to fit
forms of light and dark.

Sky, graffitied stones,
bricks too small to see—
each primitive owns
its transparency.

Eye-of-mind that skims,
mind connects the dots.
Turn until you glimpse
the Connecticut's

flow past wooded slope,
blue through forest wall's
brick-hemmed, mill-town-scoped
gaps of Turners Falls.

Once it's cut your heart,
when you've seen it bend,
think to where you're parked
at the asphalt-end.

Plein Air

Leaf-swept wisdom says,

"Older ones
    need solitude and sleep."

Like the steeple glint upon a wintry street,

as the mist
        above the glassy brook.

So do not speak,
              but leave us inside the russet nook.

The goose's wingspan
is as long as its lifespan;
where it tilts in the water,
there is no nightmare.

The surface seemed silver,
and snowflakes like memory
fell on Charles River
when we buried Gary.

The geese of this winter
have written me letters
they dipped in the river
with fingers of feathers.

Every so often
their migrating cry would
light on his coffin
of pine board and ply.

~ *In memory of Gary Ijams*

Birds Words

I

I have forgotten
whither-hither-where,
for I have gotten
assistance from the hare.

Water de-rippling
allows us to see fish again
in nearby Illinois
and a rivulet called Michigan,

And to reel in
minnow on minnow
from the star-speckled ceiling
outside our window.

II

I fear it,
just a little bit higher up,
a period
of bird sky-pileup.

Watch out!
Eared grebes like elephants
rush hour
in upper echelons

plop unexpectedly
down to the-earth-the-Lord's,
their feathers hectically
perturb the water source

wherein the vertical
must meet the filial
*making a miracle
intensely spherical.*

‘ ‘ ‘ ’ ’ ’

Say gibberish,
use warbles instead of words
at the sagebrush
assembly of the birds.

Feathery-Bird

Tail untarnished, song unheard,
I met the deep wild Feathery-Bird.
The deep wild Feathery-Bird I met
Just as the sun had almost set,
Flung by the Feathery-Bird's wild cry
Into its cradle beneath the sky.

The jungle rustles, the monsoons blow
Into wild shades where I sought to go.
Above the jungle the clouds traverse,
Full of wild fancy and poet's verse.

The resonant screeching of nature's call
Echoes like stones in the waterfall:
A crashing hellscape by life unknown,
O'er which of ancient no bird had flown,
Collapsing swiftly from overhead
Into the world of the jungle's dead.

On the border of water and earth I searched,
And found the Feathery-Bird up high.
Above the canopy, 'neath the sky,
Upon the jaggedy rock it perched,
refulgent plumage too bright to fade.

Astride through the shrubbery-root I heard
A clap of a musket, a clink of blade,
And a poacher's following threat'ning word:
"I have been in the jungle too much of late,
And my hunting only has gotten worse.
Yet I ken that this quetzal cannot escape!
I've bagged a couplet, and 'tis my third—
This tragic trappable *Feathery-Bird*."

The wild bird tottered, then flopped and flew
(I glimpsed through the gunpowder's toxic smell).
With dripping wings through the air it drew
A crimson pattern, then croaked and fell
From the tropic's canvas, without a cloud,
Into the cataract, crashing loud.

And then it was quiet. And that was all,
When the sun peeked over the waterfall.

Midnight-din
began to widow
past the hallways;

crescent-rays
inside my window
fell as always.

They were luring,
they were asking,
softly, harshly,

to a place, where,
muskrat-masking,
gasped a marshland.

It was gasping,
could you hear it?
could you stand it?

gasping sadly
for a spirit,
streetlamp-stranded.

From which teardrops
it had fluttered,
earthwards sliver,

dripping downward,
pineshaft-shuttered,
drop-sap silver.

Rawhide Flats

Go-to-bed-horse,
      you have wandered far away from your stall;
The scattered cattle-guards make it worse
      when entering an immense flat green soul.

Seeing something or other
      does not seem very far—
Colorado
      through the aperture of some barn;

                                                &

Cows' cavalcade
      over barn-boards with many holes
as a passage of souls
      to some Liminal milkmaid.

Close to Home

Lightning, charged air,
ditch road,
Holy Grail,
a vehicle with no spare—
bestowed to be there
as the black cows lowed

Quarryful,
a rippling on their ribs.

(If no Fisher King limps,
the kingfishers warble.)

Slip fast, step slow—
ice winds over the blue sea blow.

White froth, salt foam—
whitecaps upon the cold surface roam.

The mast, the snow—
hardly anyone that I know.

The heart, the soul—
two tarriers from a scattered shoal.

i

As a wave
is hurled,
we wade
in the sea
as old
as the world
was made.

ii

See
the floating graves,
Recall your childhood fears—

A whale, white in waves
appears
Out of the simmering summer sea.

iii

The sun be low,
the love be brief.
A seawave swept away my grief.

Patch
of sun,
A glitch,
line spun on gill
to catch the fish
which
he who sees is
he who seizes.

Nod atop peat,
spot a tuft of turf;
shuddering sheep's bleat
reminiscent of feet.

Feet to fare no worse,
though they stray off course
to further through bush
push away the bay
of pursuant wolf—

To say the right words.

Come sea-concealed fins,
I went up into the hill
to know where the cloud begins—
but I almost got me killed.

Of Place

Howth

Wind in the nettles a workaweek,
whale in the waves, a stripe of skies,
and the haze of an isthmus.

Bliss is conceived in the blizzard's guise.
Espy the piles of snow outside,
and wait to awake in Limerick.

Phoenix Park
For Eryn

In deer-filled Phoenix Park
I walked this way, I walked that way.
The sky was light, the grass was dark.

I met two eyes like mountain lakes.
The magpie sleeps, the magpie wakes.

Little Skelling

Hill-belaboring Irish monk,
whose eye into thy skull has sunk,
never weary, nor ever will be,
the oratory thy theory.

Erstwhile the worst isle floats,
we will row in our boats,
paddling our coracles among orcas,
an Evangelist for each of the four of us.

Skelling Michael

Twilight,
dim-lit,
not unlike
the likable.
Dolphin in an inlet,
Finian
on Skellig Michael.

Iona

Sea-lull by ten-inch sedge,
Iona ⅂ Ross of Mull—
Clouds lobbying to exchange.

Spinning and sobbing globe,
devils at pointless ploys;
Ear over-lobe-hears noise:
"saint is in Irish *noíb*".

"This wold—the All-Holder's will;
I own a monastic settlement"
said Colmcille, saint on a hill.

Yearpast dryspell doesn't matter—
sunshine cloud with wet-cloak quilted.
Rain o'er rivershore shall shatter—
not one sought it as the silt did.

What a dreary day to travel,
just Josiah, blessed Elizbeth!
Inglenook 'eese dank apparel;
tip the barrel,
since it drizzleth.

Central Midland Railway

Outside of Leicester the cows abide
by the creek of the field where the sun hangs low,
hiding their soul in their checkered hide,
not sad that the sunlight is not their soul.

Evening comes next, and a cockerel's cry
punctures our railway-ironed sky.
Sunball, a dynamite without fuse,
detonates, leaving the cows confused.

Russian Brothers Cemetery
Westford, Massachusetts

The eye looks which
way and what—
not a second summit around.

A fleeting thought,
I mistook for the skeleton of a fish
a cloud.

This wind won't stop
until it stole what it sought to steal.
See if you can understand the hill
with the water-pump tower on its top.

Halibut Point

Rockport, Massachusetts

Delicate planet,
world within *this* world—
how can something solid as granite
be this finely chiseled?

Cordoning cormorants,
concealing allness,
fog fosters formlessness
in small installments.

This butte is steep,
but consider me lucky;
Beneath my feet
naught but the pod of yucca.

Scoffing with such disdain?
And wallowing in your loaming?
Nothing is to contain,
or to escape Wyoming.

The red desert lay
coloring the unseen,
and Santa Fe
was only a fantasy.

Upon Buying a Volume of Malory in Wyoming

My lady,
I wish I went,
chere amie,
up I-25 to Cheyenne
with thee,
then tooke I-80 out West—
Cheyenne to Laramie.

In Laramie railroad rust,
like lances of knight upon knight
mistakenly thrust,
scratches the sky at night.

Near Wichita

See sandy water
emitting vapor,
the river copper,
sky partly paper.

Collapsing seldom,
cicada sentinels'
thick exoskeletons
quell a presentiment

of August's wind-gusts
and windpump-answers
above the cornhusks,
neath clouds in Kansas.

Mount Monadnock, from Bald Rock

Rocky outcrop,
verdant periphery:
the rain has stopped,
but the sides have stayed slippery.

Vultury skies
carry sparse rewards—
beginning in nosedives,
but finding trap-doors.

The feet take hold,
the eyes commune
with the rock in view,
its top intakeable.

Blesséd, anon,
is the spirit who's
content upon
Kiasticuticus.

Outlasting all bad luck,
miraclework—
it sleeps an inselberg,
wakes a monadnock.

White Mountains

The earth is the Lord's,
and so is the faint blue sky.
This is evident
when the black bird in flight
comports himself
as a migrating soul
over the alpine lakes,
then takes
a wing's-worth
of peak's-glimpse.

White, wide,
Pemigewasset's cataracts
are interminable,
full of sand shoals
impossible to placate or dislocate.
Inaccurate,
yet an analogy for a life.

May my death be
(adverbials to the verb of existence)
as a return to a rural apiary
of a deft bee,
or a flickering light in the nightly prairie,
or a downy warbler in the pinewood distance.

Ponder Assawompset

A Poem on King Philip's War

I
[Massachusetts Bay; Wamsutta's Death]

A quiet Knock-
That-Made-Me-Wake.
When I awoke,
He bade me stand.
He touched my hand
and let me look
across a Lake-
It-Had-No-End.

No sight of land
(slim crescent crust).
No shade of shore.
What's even more,
no sift of sand
(the sand got lost)

"What is this, fly southway,
if I may ask it,
elbow of Massachusetts Bay?"
It is called Nantasket.

Aggawom, northway-fly,
seeing clams get piled
under stars in the sky,
will be called Plum Island.

But Situate yourself
in Scituate itself
and see to it yourself

to sigh at the sight of sea-side Scituate,
where rays on the wave-crests scintillate.

Alexander, alas! is dead—
reap the cornhusks of grief again.
Wamsutta who waxed with war
was poisoned by Winslow's men
while hunting at Halifax;

Was marched northwards through Duxbury
      and to Marshfield against his will;
then to Massachusetts Bay Colony,
      then back to Marshfield, where he fell ill.

He, desiring
      to see Mount Hope,
died
      before he got half way home,

whence woe ghastly grew—
woman weep Weetamoe.

               Metacom,
           son of Massasoit
        (king of the Pokanoket),
next of kin to the deceased Wamsutta—
          him they instituted
            as sachem.

A sachem has so many hands.
Ceding, Philip ceded his lands.

To remedy what went wrong,
at Taunton, he turned in his guns

as one drowning, would drown in a pond.

II
[John Sassamon's Drowning; The Trial; The Hanging]

Wussausmon was a Ponkapoag
who was deft in th' Algonquian tongue,
had been picked for the Pequot War
as the English interpreter,
and did greatly aid the campaign.
Friend of Montaukett Cockenoe,
he had listened to thick blocks clack
at the printing of Holy Writ,
and the putting "I AM"
in ink—
"NEN NUTTINNIIN NEN NUTTINNIIN"—
which was dark as the quahog clam
on a backdrop of channeled whelk.

> It came as a great surprise,
> and they wouldn't have it again,
> when they found him under the ice
> at Assawompset pond.

This unsettled the Colony.

With the onset of thawing of snow,
and prolonging of hanging of sun,
comes a praying Indian; testifies

(pious convert, Patuckson hight)
Metacomet's men meted that spree
in the dead of the shivery night—

Mattachunnamo,
Wampapaquan,
& his father Tobias…

Then they laid their hands on the three.

They were brought by circuitous paths
to the Plymouth colony court,
which was stayed on a sturdy Rock.
Hour after hour elapsed,
the guilty denied their guilt,

the daylight strayed off its course,
and the courtroom began to mock.

The noiselessness needed to break,
so finally someone spoke:
We are only three Wampanoag
who stood on the shore of a lake
on a night when the ice-crust broke.

[Prosecution:] "After Lazarus' time elapsed,
the Compassionate Saviour came
as he lay in sepúlchral-clasps
to unravel his winding-lines
to deliver him out of death.

"Though this Christian was lacking fame,
the Almighty hath wrought great signs
o'er his body, bereft of breath:
Notwithstanding sufficient time
For completing the psalter-stave,
and for Maggots to glut on a flesh,
Whenever we near his grave,
he taketh to bleeding a-fresh."

Muffled noise through the witness-seats.
To assess these accurséd souls
the court-clerk scribbleth *"bleeds"*,
and a justice unwinds a scroll.

Something added, and nothing gone—
setting sun-scribe writes on and on
o'er the hill with the cows well-fed
Pharaonic Book of the Dead.

[Prosecution:] "January the twenty-ninth.
By the mercy of Jesus Christ,
the identified Christian's face
was recovered from under ice
at the shore of the white-stone-place.

"The skull had been brutally struck;
There took place a twisting of necke;
hee was stuck through a hole in the iyce
at Assawompset pond."

58

Moses muffled for Ramses' masked
pyramidical verdict asked:

light the feather, heavy the heart,
shocks, sharper than shrapnel-shard:

the heads have a place to hang.

    Tobias toppled until
    he came to his still.

      Mattachunnamo fell
      and hanged lifeless, as well.

        Tobias' son
        Wampapaquan
        was the last one in line.

          Nearing narrowing noose,
          he strained southwards to Metacom's seat

            towards the sachem who sat on Mount Hope
            in the house of Massasoit—

when the tautening cable snapped;
Wampapaquan fell on his feet
and felt the remission of rope.

III
[The War Path; The Chiasm; The Riverways]

i

By the waters the sun got soaked
muskrat-chortle through musket-choke.
On the willows we hung up our harps
red-winged blackbirds chirp.

ii

Thinning road—
we lost it,
and, as human habit has it,
Accidentally
we slept on Punkatasset.

Look, I thought
and looked around, achieving
that the Concord lights are shivering.

The vicinity conceals a shallow brook;
The extremity was starry:

Geographically a triangle,
    Boston, mount Wachusett and Monadnock
        form an obtuse angle.

iii

Crossing like souls
across the sky,
whitish clouds file
to take gray tones
above the isle.

Mendon's men's bones
lie in a pile.

iv

Rippling resumed
at the fresh-water fishing-place,

Extremal blueness of the sky
unlatch the gate,

*The Nipmuc lake
will roll its eyes and change its shade.*

v

Assawompset's icy cleft—
Sassamon's icy grave—
plunged England's colonies into death.

Yet it let the eye see in depth
through this spectacle of misfortune
*By a seawave
Him who concealed of old the pursuer-torturer.*

vi

Out of the Narragansett
into the mouth of Taunton—

incessantly row against it,
until the twine gets tautened.

At the place-where-the-fish-are,
peace-loving river opposite,
alewife-berun Nemasket—

Enter it perpendicular:
it drains into Assawompset.
Exodus, rush, and basket.

Never inquiring how,
lest you begin to doubt.

Never abandoning hope,

escape *eiskatametaupo:*

εἰς *Assabet*

κατά *Concord*

μετά *Merrimack*

ὑπό *Pemigewasset—*

Canoe across it,
where cataract-wakes won't rock it.

The case is no longer locative,
and suffixing *-ett* is foreign:

Implacable aural thorn.

vii

Time,
 rather than swim by,
settles like a bass below the ice.

Here
 in the beavery river where no sobs caught
the ear,
 I bobbed up and down in the Penobscot.

IV
[Peskeompscut; Evening]

Ebb Connecticut,
long tidal river,
and we recognize th' raggedy Peskeompscut,
at the split boulder.
The light perpetually gets older;
rain patters over the bloody eddy.

V
[Plymouth; Morning]

Sun by no sin defiled,
azure azimuth,
climbs the ladder at Plymouth,
whitewashes the shore of the Ocean where clams are piled.

It obliter-
ates stains with rays
and sifts memories
through a dune-filter.

Let's not sit there,
Let's go thither:
Far far from slaughter,
Blue blue the water.

Pietá

We always
see him on
Candlemas,

not more not less.

The elder Simeon
blessed
the baby boy who was
Ancient of Days.

The scaling foot
finds no solace;
what the sole, and what the soul is
needs no explanation.

Only a cloud, marbly put,
and warbling through an adjacent wood.

Feet are washed.
After washing they walk better,
undergone transfiguration.
Peter watched
Christ transfigurate on
Tabor.

Whilst the hillside wept with grief,
And the earthlight dressed in gloom,
I was hung beside a thief
And placed inside a narrow tomb.

The sun behind the bristle glows,
And the light in slumber lies,
Whilst the stream's low murmur cries,
Why, my son, in rest recline?
Why, my Savior, shut your eyes,
Which are cheerier than wine?

Mary of Egypt

"look at the Lord
where the stream is shallow—
you will see His reflection."

These were the words
she heard.
The Jordan was blue
at Baptism,
and the desert yellow
during the Resurrection.

Depict
the Pict.
(The Abbot is strict.)

A nasty night,
a cat on the lap,
a lot to write,
little hope to nap.

A face cannot help but yawn;
a raindrop rolled down the sun.

Tired, exceedingly tired,
he slumbered awhile by the psalterside.

Columbkille the scribe
learned that all of the dead would rise
after he saw the eyes of Christ.

Ink drips and dries
from the quiet quill.
Look at God's eyes—
they are large and still.

Imitation of Irish monastic verse

Unruffled by riff-raff waves,
which drowned sailors with their weight,
like a clear cuckoo I call
out to sea before nightfall.

Savior, steer it clear from sin,
soul in vessel that it's in.
These tear-filling eyes won't fail—
wide white ocean washing whale.

Yule,
        snuck in with Advent,
You'll
        encounter both Beginning and End.

Rabbitbrush—
        yellowish three-dimensional mesh—
ushers in a hush
        for the flesh.

Would,
        if likened to, I be considered bléssed,
this bare cottonwood,
        unwilling to let go of its swallows' nests?

Clean Monday—
the sky has been cleaned
by a loud helicopter
crossing the snowy field.

White birch,
quiet barter
with invisible merchants
at the sky-blue harbor,

Leaves lost,
branches filled up with starlings.

Foreseeing Thy divine self-emptying upon the Cross,
Habakkuk cried out, marveling.

Tranquilly quiet, truly blessed,
the grim-lipped pilgrim, who with great ease
crosses this hilly mountain crest
and directs his fish-shaped footsteps east,
suspecting the *nous*-surpassing peace
inhabits the snowy yellow grass.

Perpetuum

A quarry is out of quartz;
to awake, never even to have slept,
stepping over boards
that totter at every other step.

Somehow, the sky is key,
visible beneath a birch's arch.
It signals a glimpse of sea,
eternally enlarged.

Statues

Splintered pate;
It takes an Etruscan
to stand up straight,
since none of us can.

A leper's alone,
but you are more—
emperor,
chipped out of stone.

Easier to eschew,
harder to fathom,
the hanging Jew,
the crux of the matter.

What if
He broke the loaf
for us both,
leper and monolith?

(Old) Irish Words

"Crocaid noíb Colum Cile a corp forsna tonna glassa"

This *cloch* of stone,
This red of *derg*,
This blue of *gorm*,
This sea of *glas*—

This too shall pass.

"The wild goose
does not stop in its flight"
said the scop, kneelisome as he sat,
hinging shade with light.

"It flies over all the land
in the sight of God's face—
Who taketh thee by the hand,
and bringeth thee into a spacious place."

Perpetuum

drop a pebble in a pool,
     and the pool will ripple till
          Catskills' evening sun has cooled.
               When it hides behind the hill

The hold of the other
that cleft toward God
(the holt of the otter
left water-clogged).

Think the man weak
who lost his peace
and forsook his place
(though he makes
many knots in his sleep).

I rowed alone
under a starry ceiling;
An oar in the thole,
a thorn in my keel.

These bees,
spreading out their wings,
swarming from their hives,
Consider what has been.

Warm Lord,
teach us things
as valuable as lives.

Things seem more doable in wintertime;
the hairline of the trees recedes,
making the sky more seeable...

The height itself being invisible,
but the seeming itself more seemable.

Song of Europa

Loveable
Bovine lull.
Above all
I love a bull.

So posit if
it has become necessary to write a poem
about a random variable's second order of moment—
the probability of the probability of being positive?

Man is not a machine,
notwithstanding the mercurial radiance of his surface sheen,

nevermind that he growls with untamed ferocity,

and expects acceleration will increase velocity.

Not I'd—
if only could be inseparable from venerable Bede—abide
light-headed and headlight-eyed.

Hill, windowsill, snowfall, snowsquall.
Sick of this gossip-sickness, of spit with hyssop,
assimilate to the indivisible thickness of the hillslope.

Colorado prism

Allow:
were I a swallow,
I would not be shallow.

Rather
I'd be after
a more lofty rafter.

This prison
molts my thickest -*ism*,
and yields a different prism.

~ ~ ~

Gall, all of it:
Thy entombment,
the plea that Thy tomb be sealed.

Cows are solid,
but the mare is in movement,
as passage of wind through beetfield.

~ ~ ~

At end of summer, Advent of noises:
when hailed upon, our reservoir turquoises.

Cowpernicus

To the white-faced steer and the grass he grazes,
the mowed field is a planet; do not disturb its
bales—rectangular bumps on orbits,
neither lose sight of its changing phases.

To the white-faced sun who dries out each bale,
the steer is a speck; the mowed field, a spot on
the prairie-planet, which without fail
he illuminates lighter than cotton.

Heaven & earth are but a trick,
cirrus and prairie-flow'r persist.
Michelangelo from Sist-
-ine's cerulean must blink—

(whence even bovine pause from grazing,
flutters off road-rim meadowlark,
only the silos left unphased)
—*seeing white seam of lightning-spark.*

Maker-of-Sabbath it behooves,
nobody bruised across his path,
the Samaritan can pass
with thunder *(roll of bison-hooves).*

Starry Night Road, Owl Canyon

For Eryn neé Gammonley

"Each to each":
The remarkable hush
of this curvilinear ridge;

The cow-trough,
stars in its every inch:
the basin bathes them.

Having rolled his light-making stone
uphill, out west,
the sun must be gone. He will reappear again
a new Sisyphus.

What is art,
if not canvas-crackle
from grackle-dart?

At home the sky has grown,
as has the dome that is the flipping of a coin.

Arid although it be,
we survey tree after tree,
ever retaining hopes
of a blossoming copse.

The Beaver Pond

Warwick, Massachusetts

Only wind
strokes the cold extense of ice,
and the glint
of sunlight sweeps the woods with stinging eyes.

Sit atop the rock
that overlooks the solitary lake—
you might hear the beaver knock,
and then the snowy ice might break.

Index of Titles and First Lines

Acknowledgements

My gratitude goes to Phillip Neal Tippin for his close reading and critique of my poems, which helped transform the collection into a coherent whole. I am grateful to my father, Vladimir, and my sister, Anya, for consistently being among the earliest recipients of my new poems, and, despite their preference for Russian, graciously suffering through my English and giving me their feedback and impressions. My sense of poetry would not have developed the same were it not for the hours my father spent reading to me in childhood encouraging me to write throughout the years, and I am endlessly thankful to him for that. And finally I want to thank my loving wife Eryn, whose perception of the beauty of things has influenced and propelled my poetry since I met her.

About the Poet

Benjamin Rozonoyer grew up in Boston in a family of immigrants from the former Soviet Union. He received a masters in computational linguistics from Brandeis University, and is pursuing a PhD in computer science and machine learning at the University of Massachusetts, Amherst, while doing seasonal stunts in the industry. He currently lives with his wife and daughter in Colorado, cultivating poems and taking in local landscapes.

www.ingramcontent.com/pod-product-compliance
Lightning Source LLC
Chambersburg PA
CBHW051639120626
46551CB00014B/2138